# Koalas

by

## Gail Saunders-Smith

## Pebble Books

an imprint of Capstone Press

# Pebble Books

Pebble Books are published by Capstone Press
818 North Willow Street, Mankato, Minnesota 56001
http://www.capstone-press.com
Copyright © 1998 by Capstone Press

*Library of Congress Cataloging-in-Publication Data*
Saunders-Smith, Gail.
  Koalas/by Gail Saunders-Smith.
  p.cm.
  Includes bibliographical references (p. 23) and index.
  Summary:  Describes and illustrates various
activities of koalas and their joeys.
  ISBN 1-56065-486-4
  1.  Koala--Juvenile literature. 2. Koala--Infancy--Juvenile
  literature. [1.  Koala.  2.  Animals--Infancy.]  I.  Title.

QL737.M384S38  1997
599.2'5--dc21
                                    97-8307
                                     CIP
                                      AC

**Editorial Credits**
Lois Wallentine, editor; Timothy Halldin and James Franklin,
design; Michelle L. Norstad, photo research

**Photo Credits**
Bob Bowdey, cover, 4, 6, 10, 18
Visuals Unlimited/Will Troyer, 8; Carlyn Galati, 3, 12;
  Kjell B. Sandved, 1, 14; Ken Lucas, 16; Cheryl Hogue, 20

2

# Table of Contents

3

A koala
climbs up trees.

A koala eats eucalyptus leaves.

8

A koala sleeps on high branches.

A koala has babies.

# Babies are called joeys.

14

A joey rides
on backs.

A joey learns
to climb up trees.

A joey learns
to eat eucalyptus
leaves.

A joey learns
to sleep on high
branches.

# Words to Know

**branch**—a part of a tree that grows out of its trunk like an arm

**joey**—a young koala

**koala**—a small, furry animal that lives in trees; it is found in Australia

**leaves**—the flat and usually green parts of a plant or tree

# Read More

**George, Linda.** *The Koalas of Australia.* Mankato, Minn.: Hilltop Books, 1998.

**Powzyk, Joyce.** *Wallaby Creek.* New York: Lothrop, Lee and Shepard Books, 1985.

# Internet Sites

**About Koala—Cuddly, Stubby Little Australian Marsupial Animal**
http://ozramp.net.au/~senani/koala.htm

**Koala's Page**
http://www.geom.umn.edu/~jpeng/KOALA/
koala.html

**Lone Pine Koala Sanctuary — Koala Information**
http://www.koala.net:80/animals/koalas.htm

**Species Facts: Koala**
http://www.lpzoo.com/animals/mammals/
facts/koala.html

**The Australian Koala Page**
http://www.aaa.com.au/Koala.html

## Note to Parents and Teachers

This book describes and illustrates several behaviors of koalas and their cubs. The clear photographs support the beginning reader in making and maintaining the meaning of the text. The sentence structure provides practice for the child to assume more control of the text. Children may need assistance with the expository vocabulary. Children also may need assistance in using the Table of Contents, Words to Know, Read More, Internet Sites, and Index/Word List sections of the book.

## Index/Word List

*Word Count: 45*

24